The Flight of a Dragonfly

A Collection of Tanka and Cherita Poems

Ram Chandran

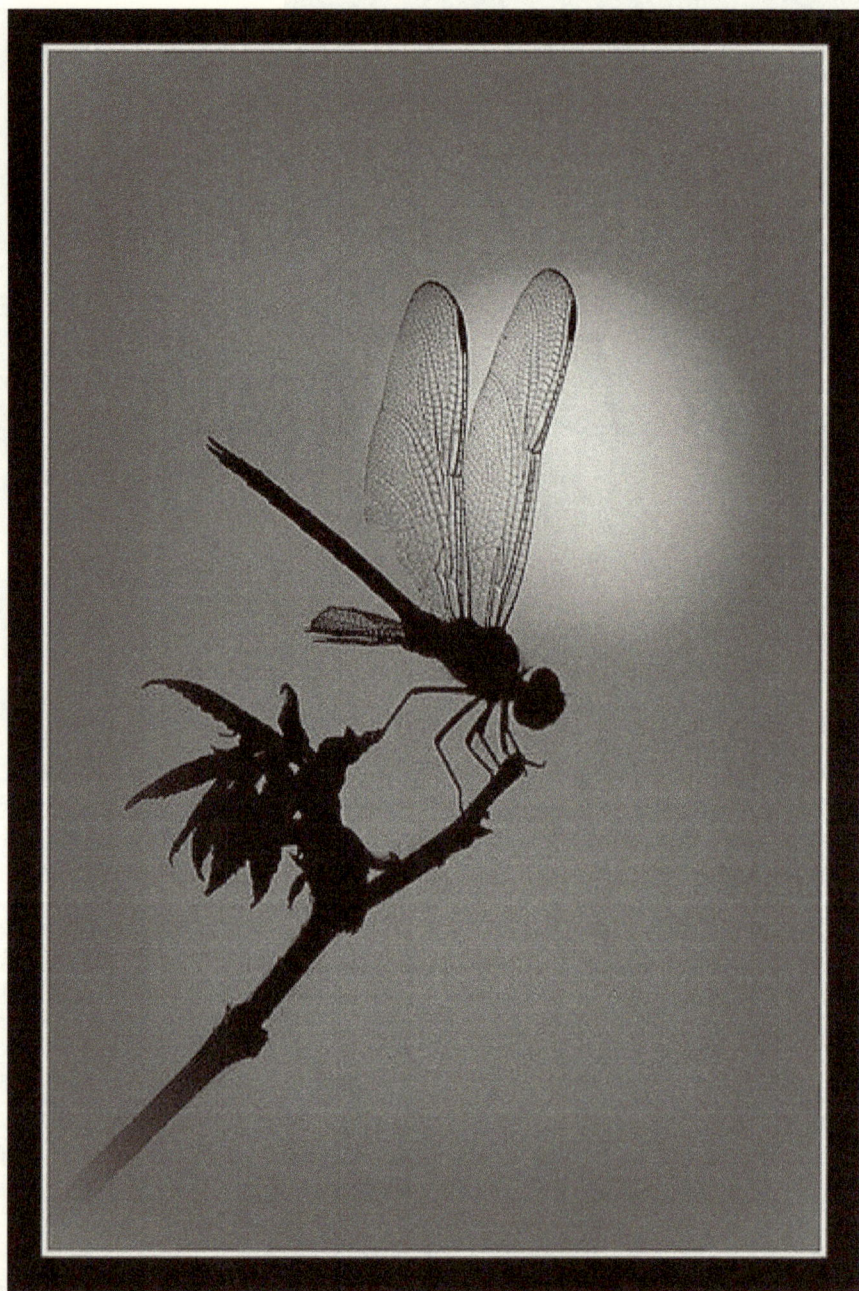

The Flight of a Dragonfly

A Collection of Tanka and Cherita Poems

Ram Chandran

The Flight of a Dragonfly

By Ram Chandran

First Edition

Author: Ram Chandran
Editor: Paul Gilliland
Formatting: Southern Arizona Press
Cover Artwork: *Dragonfly* by Kono Bairei c.1895
Interior Artwork: Pixabay and Create Vista

Published by Southern Arizona Press
Sierra Vista, Arizona 85635
www.SouthernArizonaPress.com

ISBN: 978-1-960038-20-3

Poetry

Dedication

To my daughter, Nithya.

Tanka Poems

as I walk
a nameless bird
on a nameless tree
flies away suddenly
leaving me all alone

when
the night is so l o n g
and even cicadas are asleep
in my solitude
I long for your warm hug

her smile
at me, a jasmine blossom
I am sure
she's opening
a new chapter in my life

parched my heart
in this l o n g monsoon night ...
by fireside
the flames dance to the tune
of my solo songs

Ram Chandran

lots of differences
this moon
from my childhood moon;
my mom whispered
when I met her last

leaning
on her shoulder
I point to a distant star
as she draws
star on beach sands

red hibiscuses
outside hospital windows
sway -
drop by drop
blood transfusion

when I kiss her
under the shadow of a moonlit tree
falling flowers
from swaying branches ...
and stars inside my shut eyes

sitting alone
under a maple tree
I
talk with
the fallen leaves

ikebana —
however I arrange the flowers
I
always feel
a flower is missing

like the hues of grey
between
black and white
I am
and I am not

hey
give me the wings
to fly
and brush the moon
with a riot of colour

that day
when we first met in twilight
and now
when we depart into shadows ...
the same moon

I fly
with birds
dream
with stars
and go with sun

one
after another
the falling leaves ...
my trembling hand
picks one

come, kiss me hard
once before you go
in search of mountain peaks
and ocean depths ...
for, you may dissolve there forever

gardening scissors -
I cut
my
problems
to size

sailing
thousands of miles
oh clouds
take me
along with you

Ram Chandran

parched
my heart, even in these
monsoon times ...
my unsung songs
the rain washes away

the whistle
of a distant train
reminds me
the journeys
I have not started

waves
raise beautiful blue walls
and smash it ...
like you sow dreams
in me and shatter them

as breeze
caresses long hair,
she
tosses her head
and my heart too

Ram Chandran

on a monsoon day
when everywhere rain sings,
from the neighbour's tree
a cuckoo's song
exclusively for me

do not
touch and go
like a wave
flow through me
like the breeze

cloudy sky
no stars to count
my insomnia
and infinite
thoughts of you

I
have nothing to say
except
what is said in all these years
in my silence

moon plays
hide and seek with clouds -
the truth
and falsity
of our conversation

twilight -
suddenly
branches of the tree
he planted years ago
stopped quivering

winter moonlight
my songs go unheard
through the bamboo tree ...
a distant cowbell
echoes my songs

once
walking
along the towpath
I lost my way back home ...
forever

smoke
from the chimney
merges with morning mist ...
a pot of hookah
for the old fisherman

slowly goes
like a dream, a fantasy
an illusion …
the path I tread
the life I lived

in this quiet noon
on this shore
my tied boat
me
and a seagull

jasmine
in bloom overnight
I need
nothing else
for the day

only
the moonlight knows
the tears
that flowed down my cheeks
the sleepless nights I have spent ...

a little ghost
in the banyan tree
scares all
in the village, friends with birds
and swinging on aerial roots

Ram Chandran

on the seashore
waves
repeatedly bring
those bitter memories
the breeze takes them away

though you pretend
not to hear,
my Radhe
your jingling bangles
echo my songs

silent mountain
murmuring trees
... the stream
lost in the woods,
me too

fading out
the folk music
as the caravan moves on
camels footprints
and my mind stay behind

flowing
miles and miles
this river
still conceals
a bit of the mountain

by fireside,
I threw my
unadulterated dreams
one by one ...
anosmia

and finally
all I want is -
a beach hut
a little sushi to eat
and lots of stars in the sky

like sunrise
and sunset
I will come
and go
again and again

she breathed her last -
outside the window
rests
on a flower
a fluttering butterfly

sailing
towards the thin line
where sea meets the sky ...
the boatman's love song
winds carry to his lonely bride

her
kajal lined
blue eyes ...
it's dreams and dreams
floating inside

edge of the lake
the repeated lap
of waves
go up and down
the heron's leg

Ram Chandran

Cherita Poems

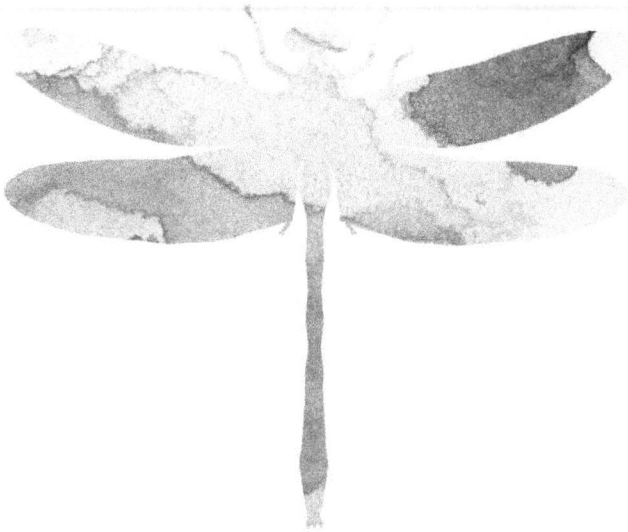

Ram Chandran

a mountain meadow flower

no one
knows its name

still I preserve it
just in memory
of the mountain

spreading its shine

on a fir tree,
a snowflake
a jasmine

and on me ...
the same moon

morning mist

tied boat
dancing to the waves …

with a pot of hookah
the old fisherman
in a musing mood

still night

stars
one by one
slip into the pond

moon
follows

a colourful feather
of an unknown bird

drifts,
sways
floats ...

in the winds ...

moonlit sky

for each star
that sparkles
up in the sky

in my garden
a parijat replica

(Parijat, night-jasmine in English, literally means celestial. Parijat bloom at night and fall down in the morning.)

Ram Chandran

a mountain stream

in deep
dark woods

your thoughts
run through
my veins

stars in the sky

fireflies
over
the paddy fields ...

walking a narrow path
to heaven

Ram Chandran

seagulls
fly joyously
over the shore

faraway
a thin line ...

sea meets the sky

moonless sky

too dark in the woods
even for the night birds

fireflies
sprinkle
magical light

children's park
isolated corner bench

fallen maple leaves

waiting
for an old friend
with his grandson

a walk
along the river

remembering
those days
when we were together

under a falling star

Ram Chandran

monsoon ...

all over the sky
dark black clouds

as the rain begins
I close my book
and sing with rain

mesmerising

this jasmine
just pure white

lifting
the fragrance,
the evening breeze

Ram Chandran

awestruck

at page number 58
for last two hours ...

outside the window
the magic
of winter moon

pitch dark
sudden lightning –

forest path
stretches
a few yards

pitch dark again

gusty winds

sweep
all the leaves ...

my
shadow
under the tree

sitting on the bund

searching
a pebble

to throw
in the pond ...
with my dreams

Ram Chandran

autumn winds

ripples
of lush green paddy fields

merge
into the distant
low hanging moon

slowly climbing up ...

as I
dissolve
into the mountain mists

my dreams
flow down the stream

I
me
myself

and silence

life goes on
in another world

About the Author

Ram Chandran is a Corporate Lawyer by profession. He has been writing English poems since his college days and has written poems and short stories in many literary magazines. A haijin since 2020, he has written more than 1200 Japanese short form poems.

His Tanka, haiku/senryu and Cherita have been published in reputed Haiku magazines both print and digital including *Modern Haiku, The Heron's Nest, Kingfisher Journal, The Cicada's Cry, Wales Haiku Journal, Failed haiku, Tsuri-doro, World Haiku Review, The Mainichi, Haiku Dialogue, The Bamboo Hut, Stardust Haiku, haiku kontinuum, Take 5ive Journal, Scarlet Dragonfly Journal, Ribbons-Tanka Society of America, Presence haiku journal, Ourbesthaiga, MoonInk,* Haiga *Galleries of The Haiku Foundation, WHITE ENSO, Tandem, The Rengay Journal, Prune juice, Chrysanthemum,* and *The Cherita.com.*

Follow on Instagram at: haiku_ram_chandran

Acknowledgements

Cold Moon Journal

Moonink Poetry, an anthology of contemporary Tanka poetry

Ourbesthaiga

Presence, Britain's leading independent haiku journal

Ribbons-Tanka Society of America Journal

Scarlet Dragonfly Journal

Take 5ive Journal

The Haiku Foundation, Haiga Galleries

The Cherita, Home of Cherita